What a DAY!

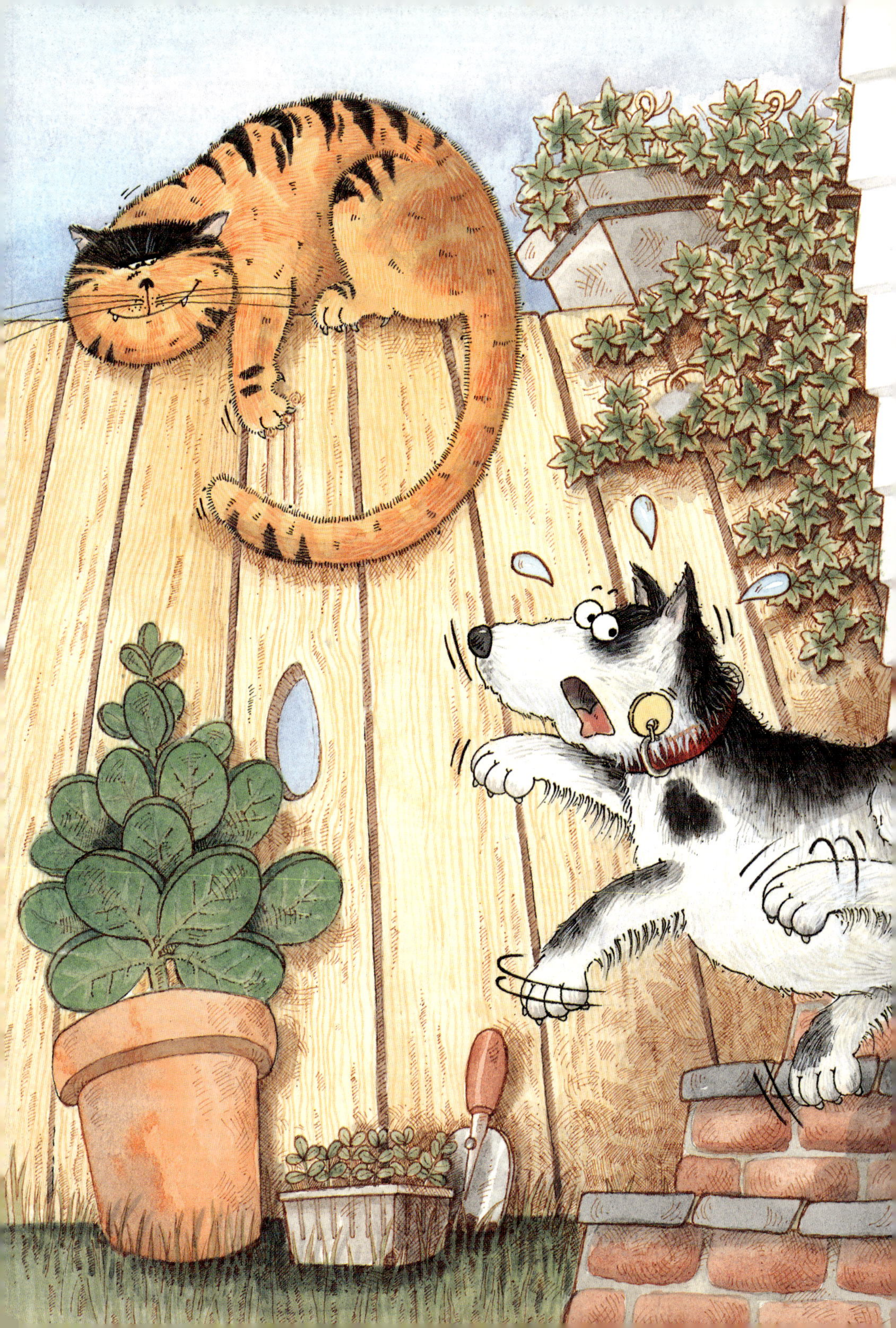

It started this morning when the old rooster down the road crowed. Well, any dog who calls himself a dog would have to take up a challenge like that, wouldn't he? I made a dive for the dogflap in the kitchen door. I was just launching into my most deepthroated, threatening *woo-woo-woof*, guaranteed to scare the tail feathers off any rooster, when somehow I got my tail caught in the flap as it swung shut. My *woo-woo-woof* turned into an *ow-wow-wow*.

    That sort of thing makes a dog feel rather silly. I was licking my poor tail when I heard a snigger. I looked up and — wouldn't you know it? *That* creature from next door was perched on the garden fence, with its tail in a half hoop and its whiskers folded back. It smirked, "Nice morning."

Think of it! *Me!* Being nice-morninged by The Mean Monstrosity. Just as if he hadn't seen me with my tail stuck in the door! Now, no dog who calls himself a dog can stand a smirking cat, so I leapt at the fence.

I never thought I'd reach him. I never have

before. So when I wound up with a long hairy tail-tip in between my teeth, I didn't know who was more shocked, The Mean Monstrosity or me!

Eeyowffftttzz! bawled The Mean Monstrosity. It really would have put my teeth on edge if they hadn't already been busy with the tail.

Of course, when I dropped back onto the ground, The Mean Monstrosity landed on top of me with all his claws stuck out. He spat in my eye. I snapped at his nose. Then we settled down to ignore each other and attend to our injured tails.

    I was quietly picking the fur out from between my teeth when The Mean Monstrosity's Missus came racing out in her dressing gown and tried to clip me over the nose with a newspaper. No dog who calls himself a dog can stand for that sort of thing, so I headed for my dogflap. As I went, I heard The Mean Monstrosity giving a small cattish snigger.

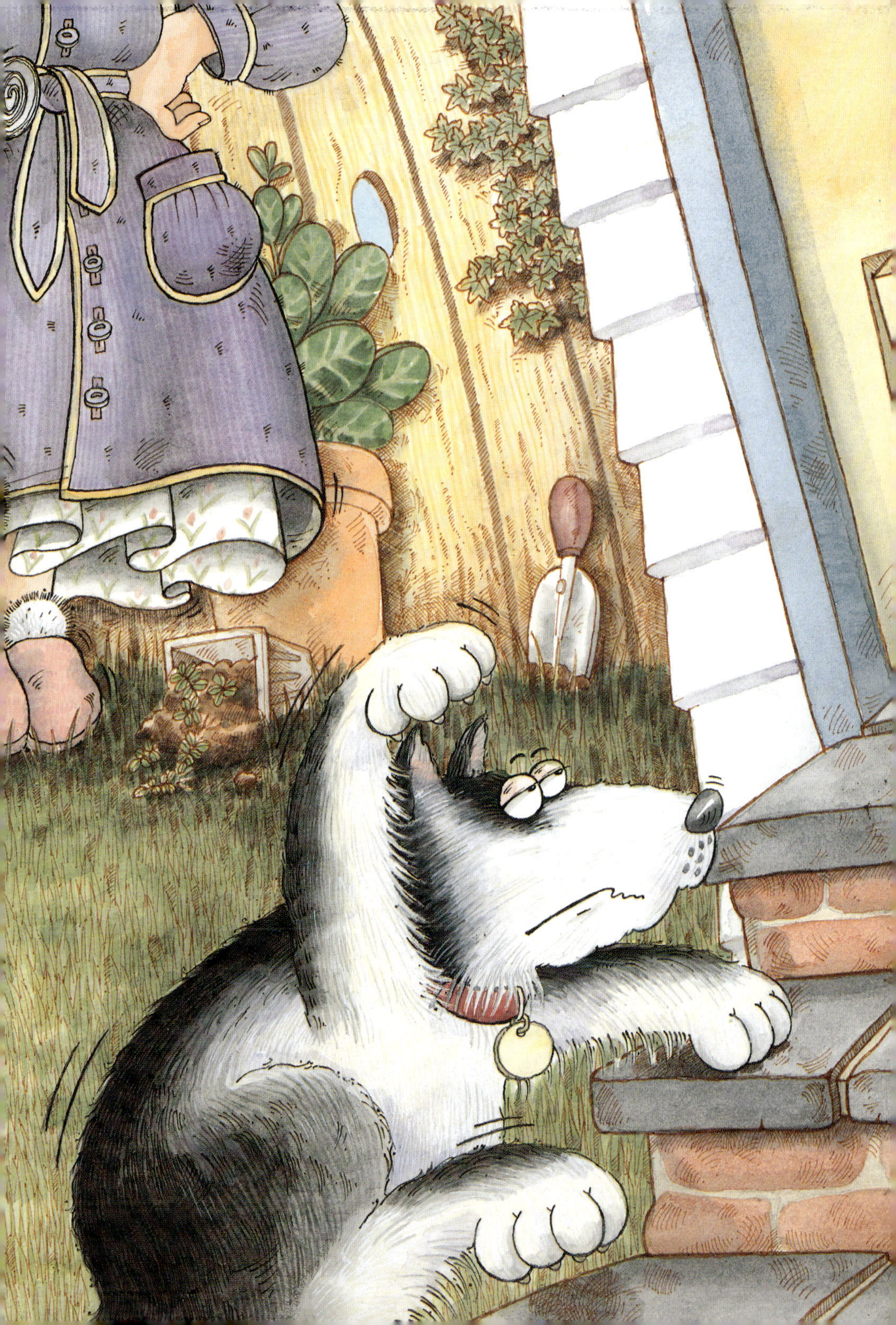

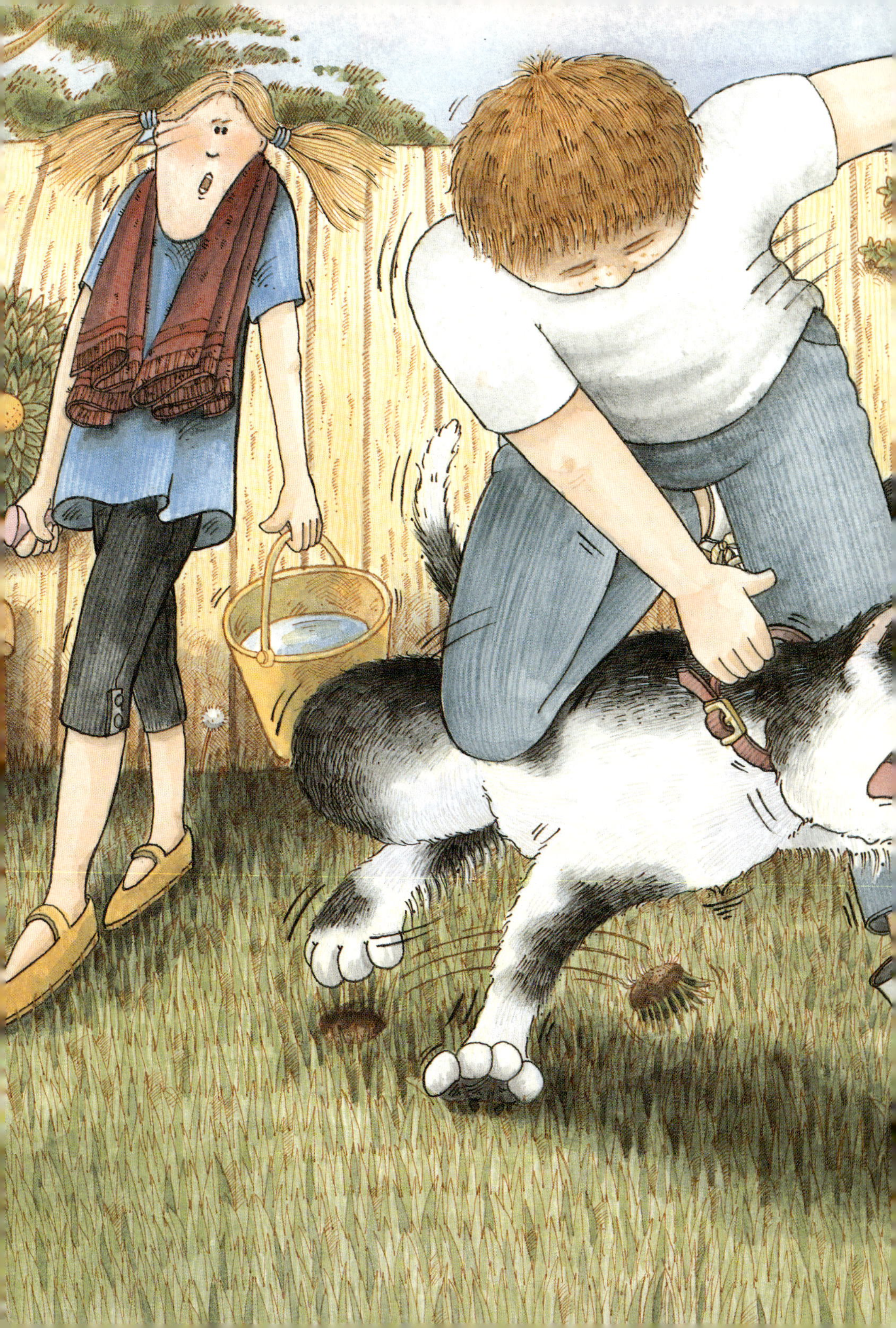

I settled in my kitchen until the family got up. Things were all right until after breakfast, when The Kids took me out into the garden. I thought we might be going to play *rabbits-in-the-bushes* or something like that, so I went along with them. Then one of those traitors held me by the collar while the other one brought out a bucket of warm water, a bar of flea soap, and a towel. No dog who calls himself a dog can put up with that, so I twisted away from the one that was holding me and shot under my favorite bush.

It was a bit prickly under there but nice and safe, so I scraped myself a shallow hole to lie in. I thought I'd stay in there until they were tired of looking for me and then sort of ease out as if I'd never been gone.

It didn't work. One of The Kids got hold of my poor tail and the other one got my hind legs and they hauled me backwards out of the bush. I tried to use my front claws as brakes, but it didn't help. Nothing helped.

They tied me up to the fence and tipped that whole bucket of water over me. Then they lathered me from my ears on back. Oh, the indignity! They got another bucket of water and threw that over me, too. Then they scrubbed at me with that old towel.

I sat down and shook as pathetically as I could, which wasn't difficult as the warm water soon got cold after it was out of the bucket. I sneezed a couple of times and scrubbed my nose with my front paws.

"Poor Mr. D," said one of The Kids. "He's cold. We'd better let him have a run to dry off."

"All very well," I thought, "but who made me wet in the first place?"

"I'll get him some Doggities," said the other one. So they untied me and went away. I shook myself thoroughly and rolled in the grass. The Kids came back with my dish full of Doggities *and* a wonderful big beef bone! I hadn't seen such a big bone for ages so I wagged my tail. The day had begun to look up. "Good dog," said The Kids. Then away they went, swinging the bucket and towel and smelling as strongly of flea soap as I did.

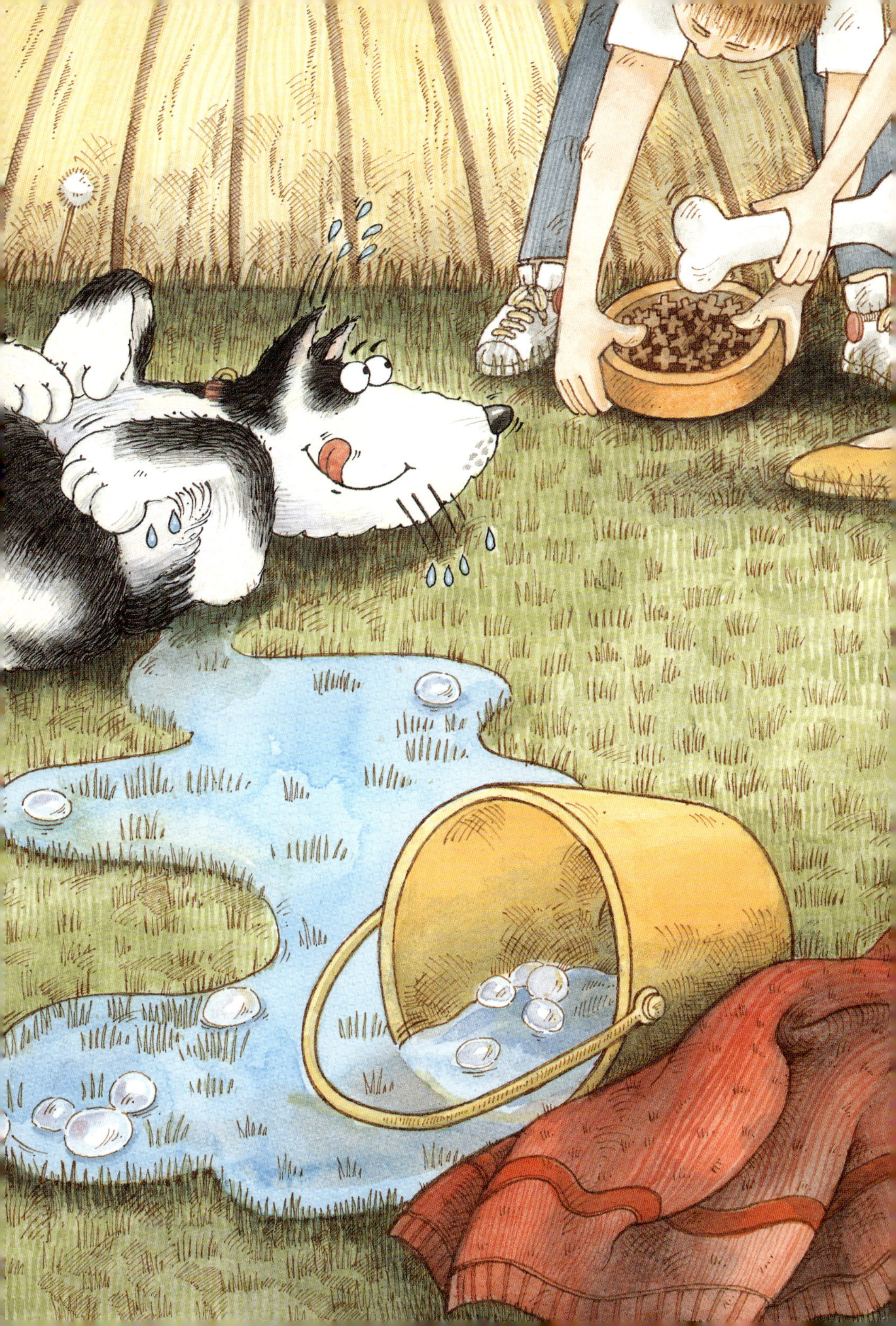

I picked up the bone and set it between my front paws. Then I heard a low growl and looked up — right into the mean eyes of The Walking Dogfight, who lives two houses down the road. The Walking Dogfight wanted the bone. *My* bone. Now no dog who calls himself a dog would give in to that. (That's why I don't call myself a dog anymore.) I let him have it. After all, The Walking Dogfight is a cross between a bull terrier and a goodness-knows-what, and he looks like it.

He pushed open the gate, grabbed my bone and then just stood looking at me with a sparkle of triumph in those reddish eyes. He'd known all along I'd give him the bone. Oh well, I still had my Doggities to eat. I turned around and saw another ghastly sight. The Mean Monstrosity was crouching over my plate with his tail wrapped around his haunches, and he was crunching Doggities. *My* Doggities. "Thanks for the meal," said The Mean Monstrosity. He got up and stretched. "Did you enjoy your bath?"

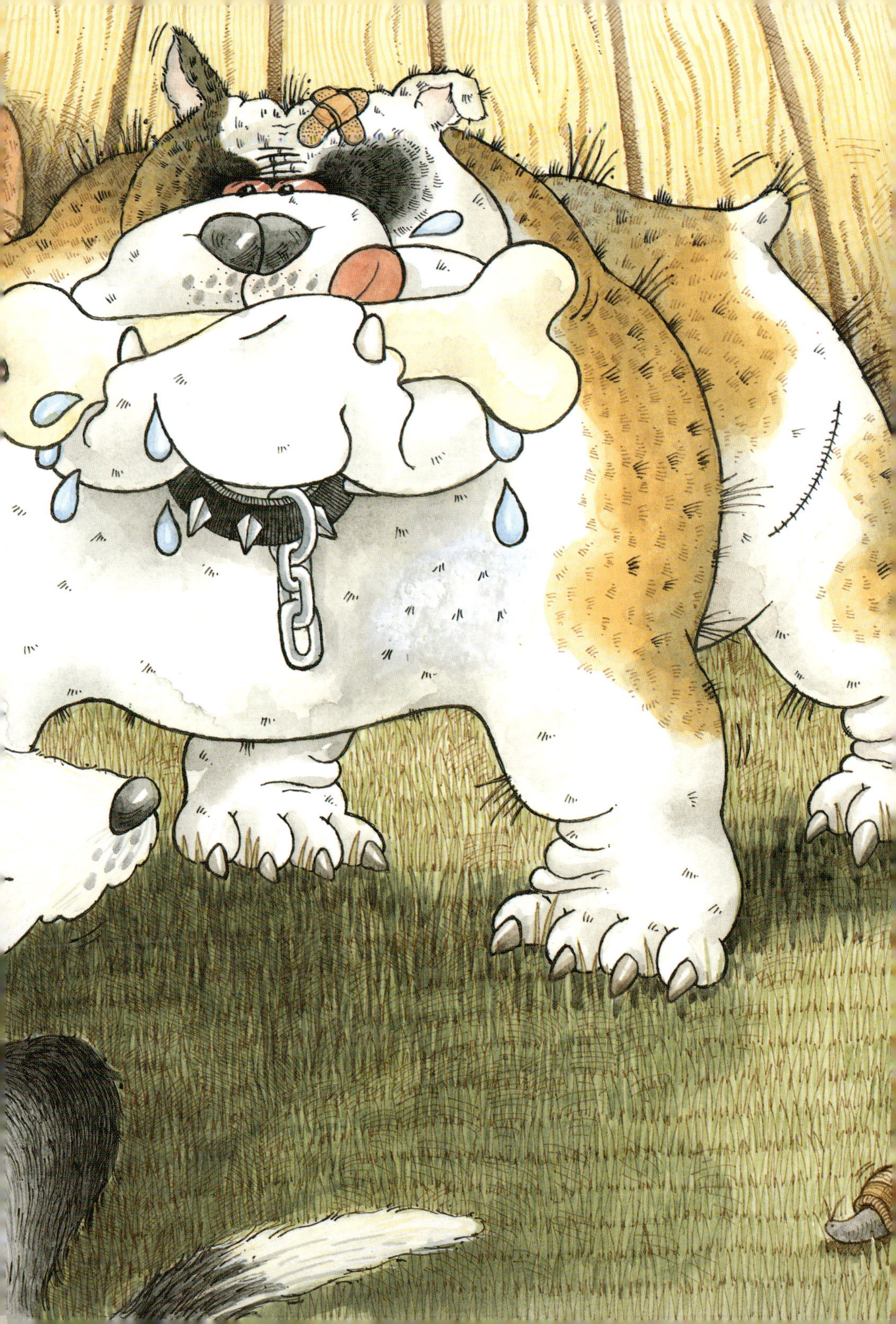

Then he mooched across the lawn and hopped back over the fence.

I slunk back into the house with my tail between my legs and collapsed under the table. A car came up the driveway and stopped, but I didn't even bark at it. That was how down I was feeling!

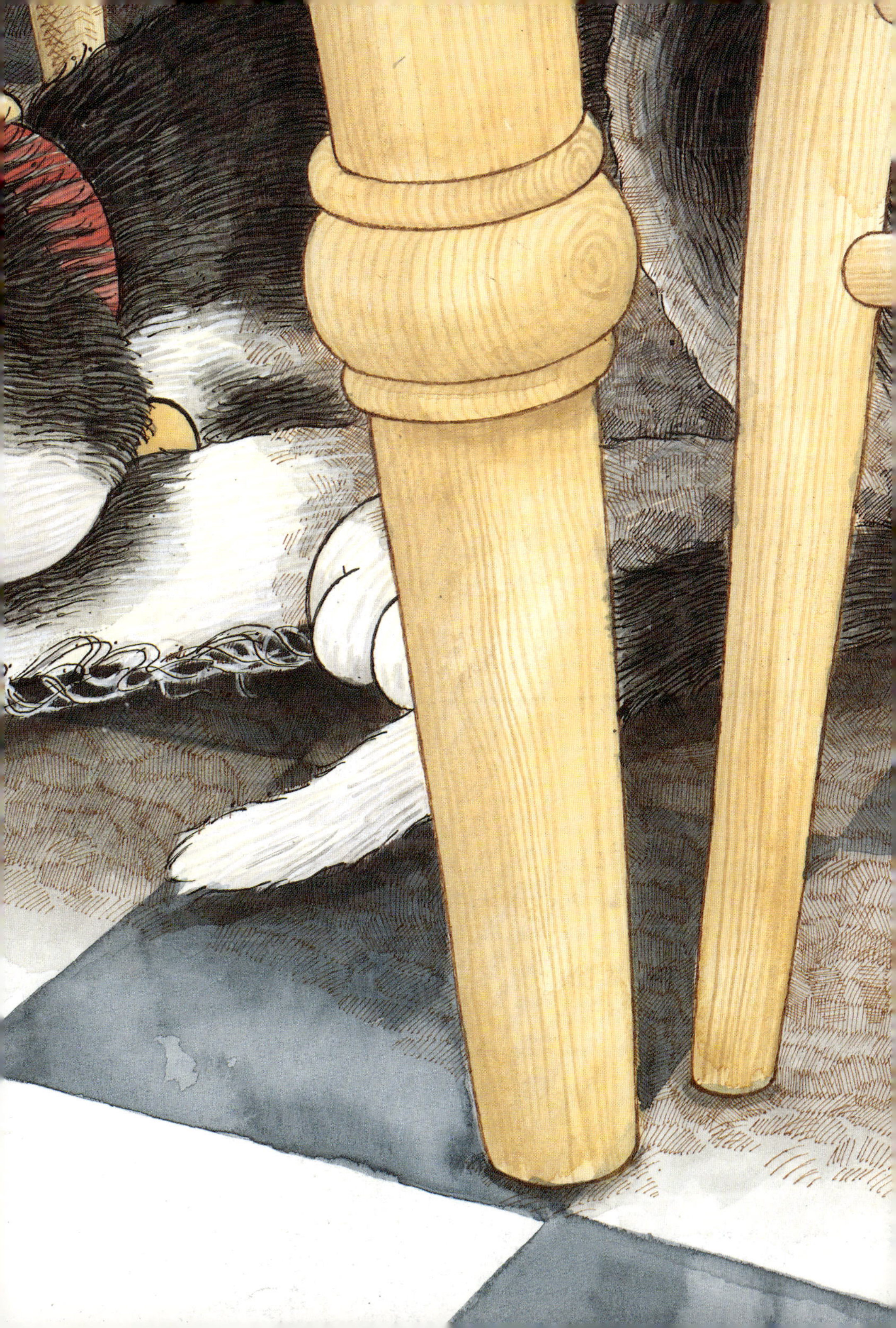

My Missus opened the door and let in a woman and a little boy. He was a nice little boy, just at the crumb-dropping stage. I hung around hopefully while my Missus made a pot of tea. Out came the cookies and she gave one to the little boy. He made plenty of crumbs all right, and I licked them up. Then he broke off a corner of cookie and dropped that. I wagged my tail. Children like that. He held out the rest of the cookie, and I took it politely and crunched it up. And that's when my nice little boy started to yell and tried to grab the cookie out of my mouth!

My Missus gave the little horror another one and put me out in the garden. It wasn't fair, so I squeezed under the gate to run away. I was half under when I saw the front feet and huge jaws of The Walking Dogfight. I tried to back up and found I couldn't. My collar was hooked at the bottom of the gate. There I was, flat on my belly with my nose in the mud. I tried to bark but it came out as a strangled yap.

"Be quiet, Mr. D!" yelled my Missus.

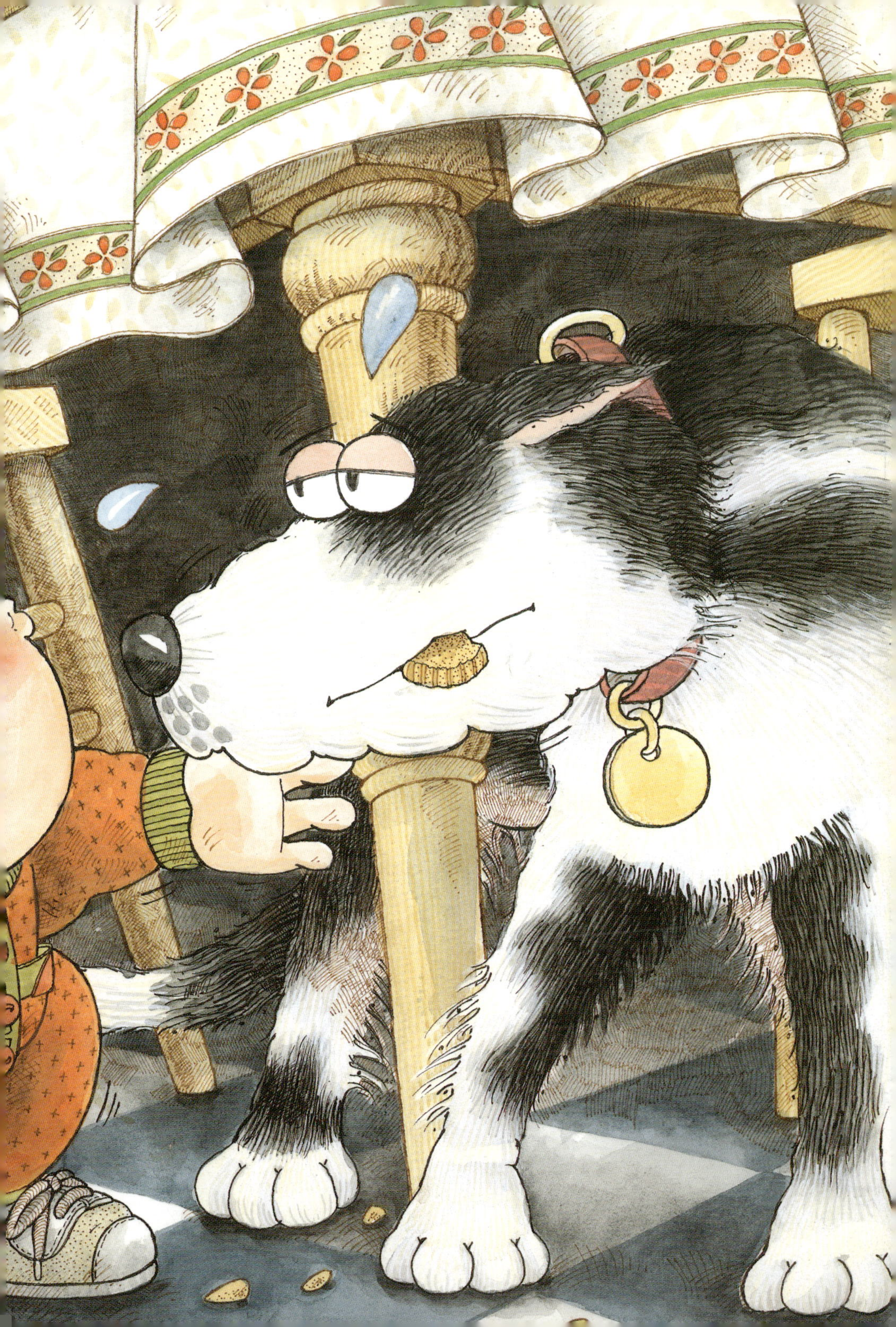

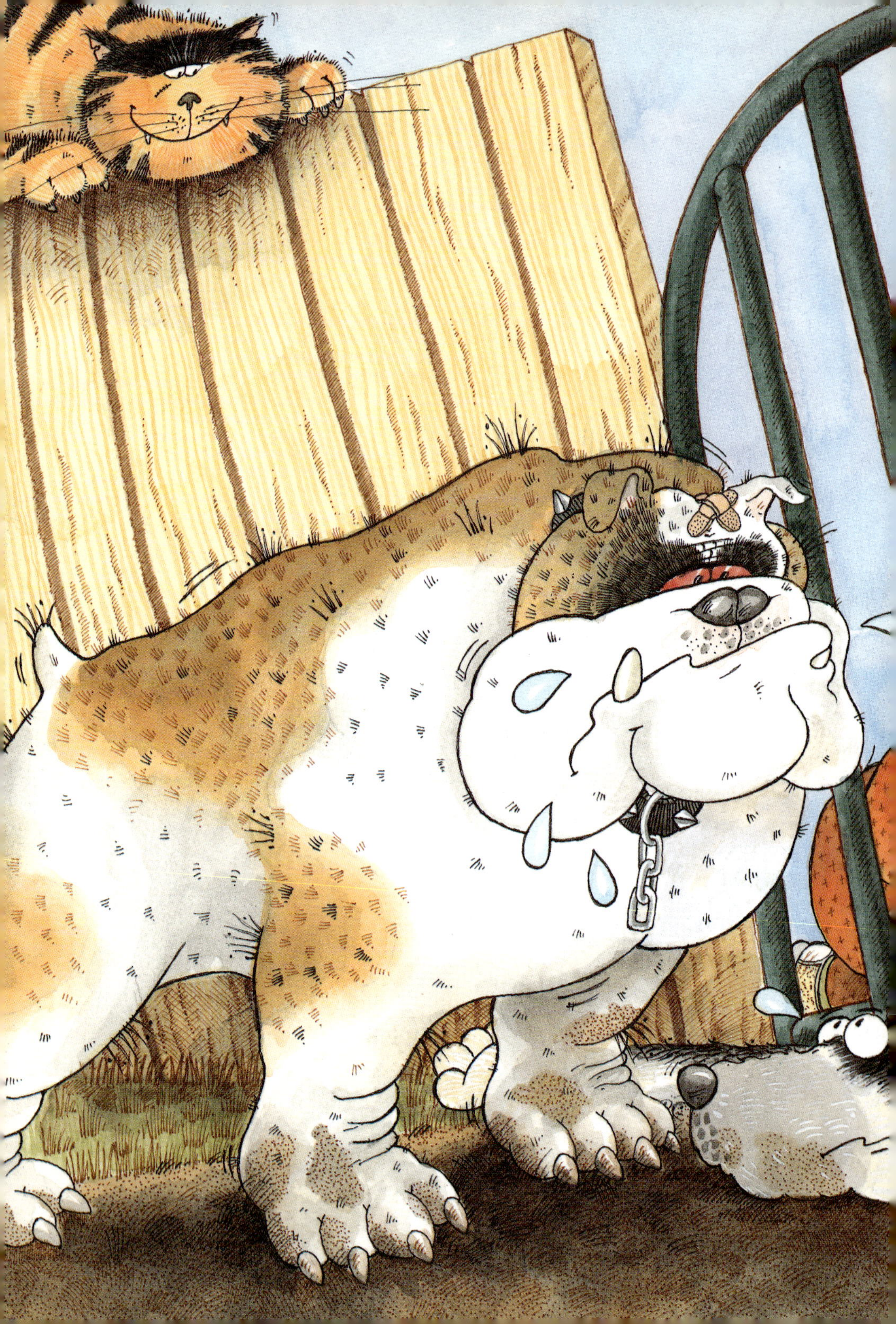

The little boy must have crawled out of the dogflap because he came over and squatted down beside me. He pointed at my ear and said, "Deee!" and then he pulled my tail. I tucked it under me. When he started pulling my eyebrows, I couldn't stand it. Not with The Walking Dogfight watching. I snarled. That did it.

My Missus and the other woman came out, grabbed the little boy, unhooked me from the gate, and tied me up again. I looked about and — you've guessed it — there was The Mean Monstrosity perched on the fence. Smirking. He must have been there the whole time. "Just hanging about, Mr. D?" he asked. Then The Walking Dogfight looked his way and he sort of flowed off the fence and away across his own garden.

I lay down and put my chin on my paws. I could have howled, but what would that get me? More smart remarks from The Mean Monstrosity? More stony glares from The Walking Dogfight?

What a day!

Reckon that was the end? Well, it wasn't. Sometime in the afternoon I was woken up by The Kids. They untied me and then brushed me all over and even hauled a comb through the long hair of my legs. "There," said The Girl Kid. "Now you look very handsome, Mr. D. Let's get you dressed up."

Well, I didn't like the sound of that much. When The Kids were younger, they were always dressing me up in things and pretending I was a teddy bear.

"What'll we put on him?" asked The Boy Kid.

"Crepe paper," said The Girl Kid, and she cut out some long bits of stretchy, colored paper. The Kids tied it all over me — around my tail and legs and even around my collar.

"That'll do," said The Boy Kid, tying a knot. "Let's get going."

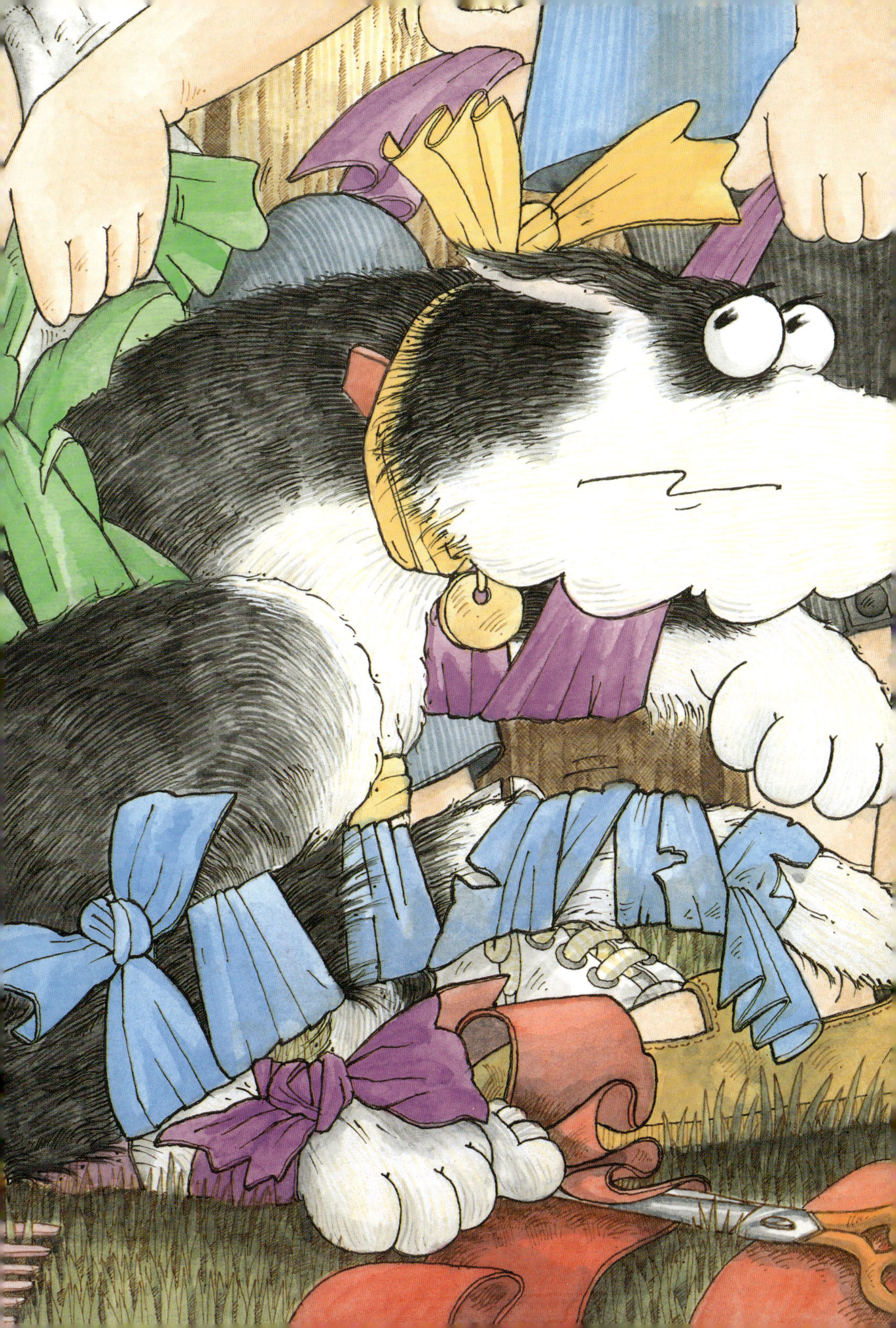

I didn't know where we were going, but you can bet I didn't want The Mean Monstrosity or The Walking Dogfight to see me done up like this! While we waited at the corner for the green light, I chewed some of the paper off my tail. Then I pretended I had a flea and scratched my ears with my hind foot. That shifted a bit more of the stuff.

"Stop that, Mr. D!" said The Girl Kid, jerking my leash.

We went across the road, and I swiveled my

eyes around a bit. I used my ears. Odd, I couldn't hear a cattish snigger anywhere. I couldn't hear the splodgy pawsteps of The Walking Dogfight either. Maybe I was going to be lucky!

At the next set of lights, I scratched with the other hind foot and chased another imaginary flea with my teeth. Now all that was left was the colored paper around my collar, and I didn't have a chance to get at that. We'd run out of corners.

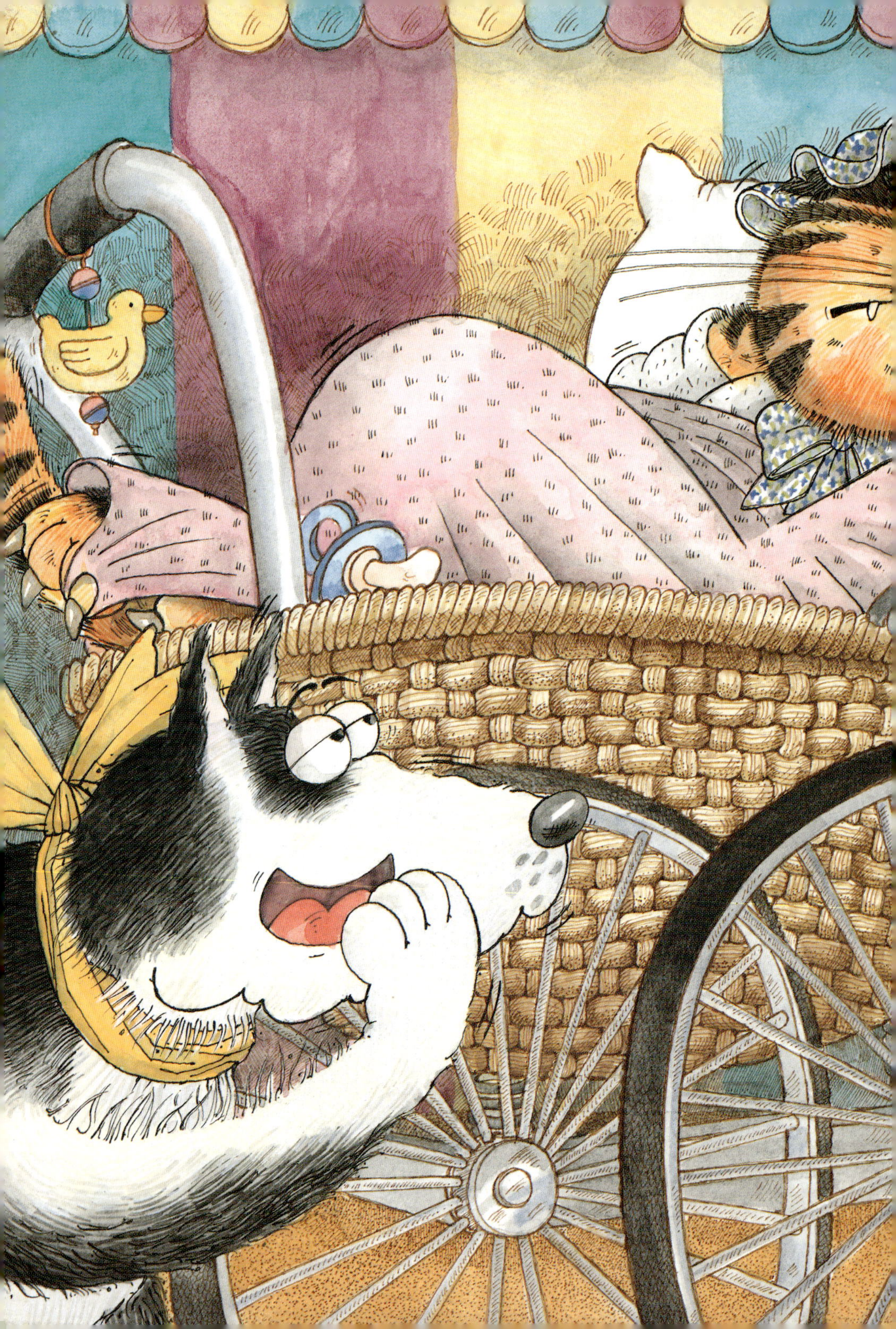

Well, in the end we reached the park. There was something going on there. I could see tents and people and big shiny silver things. One of the silver things was yelling.

"There, I told you we'd be late," said The Girl Kid. "Now we haven't got time to fix Mr. D up again." She hauled me into a big circle with white posts around it.

"Class 3 for the Best Decorated Pet!" yelled the silver thing again. It was quiet for a minute or two; then I heard a noise I'd heard before. *Woooooeeeeee!* it went. Oh no, I thought, and tried to hide behind a post. Only one creature yelled like that. It had to be The Mean Monstrosity. Oh, the shame of it! The Mean Monstrosity to see me like this! I heard the wail again and I opened one eye. Then the other one. And I knew I didn't have to worry too much! You should have seen him! Imagine! The Mean Monstrosity, terror of the neighborhood, scourge of the local cats, persecutor of Mr. D — dressed up as a baby in a baby carriage! If I hadn't heard that yowl I wouldn't have recognized him. His ears were crammed under a bonnet and he had a woolly thing around his top half. The rest was under a blanket. I stared. The Mean Monstrosity stared back.

Then something else happened. Slowly, dragged step by dragged step, something was being hauled into the ring. It was dressed up in a blue jacket with blue trousers and it had a sort of hat on its head. A bit of white tail stuck out the back and two red eyes glittered at the front. The Walking Dogfight!

28

If I had time I'd tell you about how The Mean Monstrosity finally got out of the baby carriage and The Walking Dogfight got disqualified for chewing up the microphone. The way it all ended was in the biggest free-for-all I've ever seen. Oh yes, I saw it. No dog who calls himself a dog would get mixed up in a thing like that!

The Kids brought me home, and I can see The Boy Kid coming toward me with another big bone. The Walking Dogfight has just slunk past, practically down on his belly with shame. And I thought I saw one black ear poking over the fence a few minutes ago. Just you wait till tomorrow when I see The Mean Monstrosity. "Hey, Kitsyboy!" I'll say. "And how's Mommy's Diddums today?" That should fix *him* for a while. But for now, I'll just eat this delicious beef bone — excuse me — *mmmmm*, wonderful things, beef bones…

What a day!

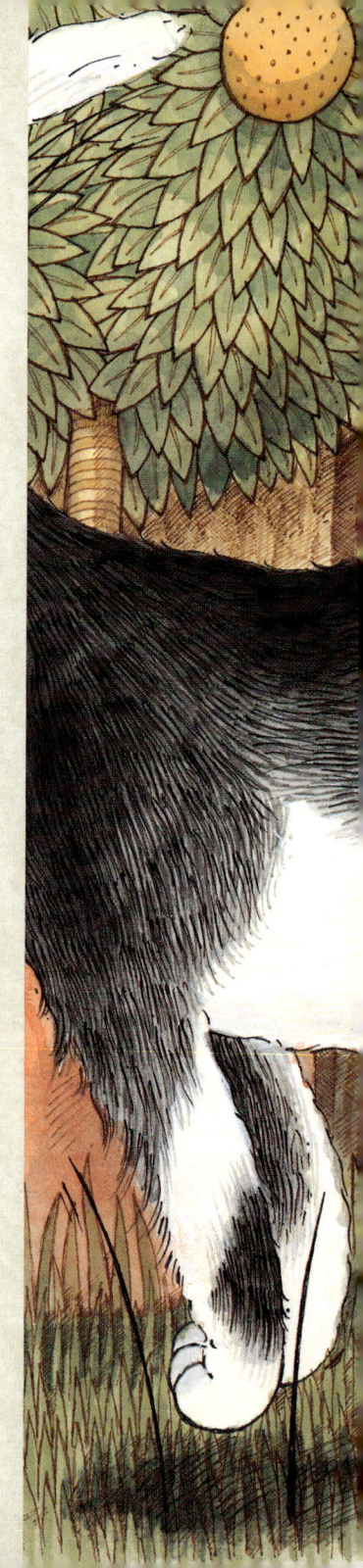

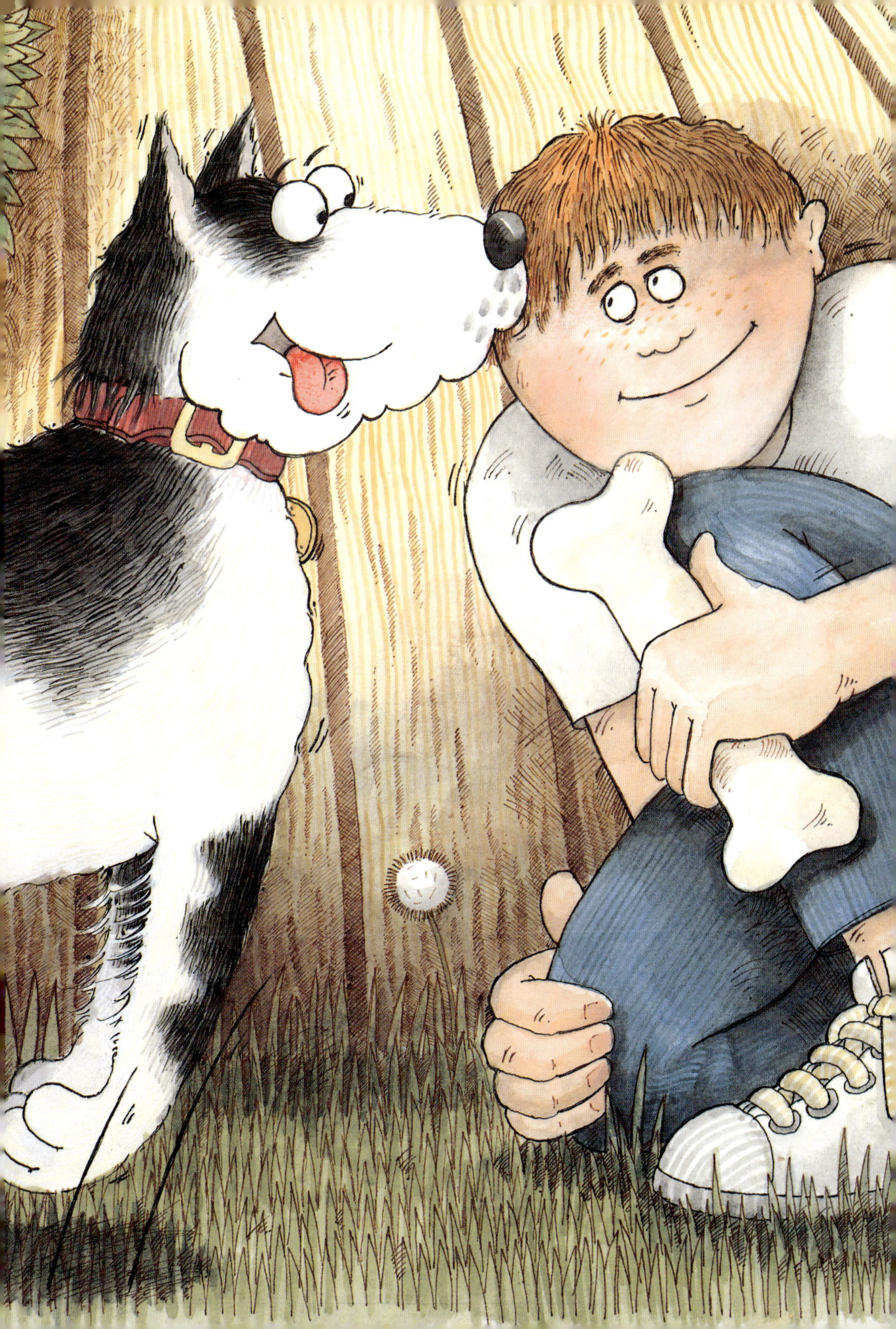

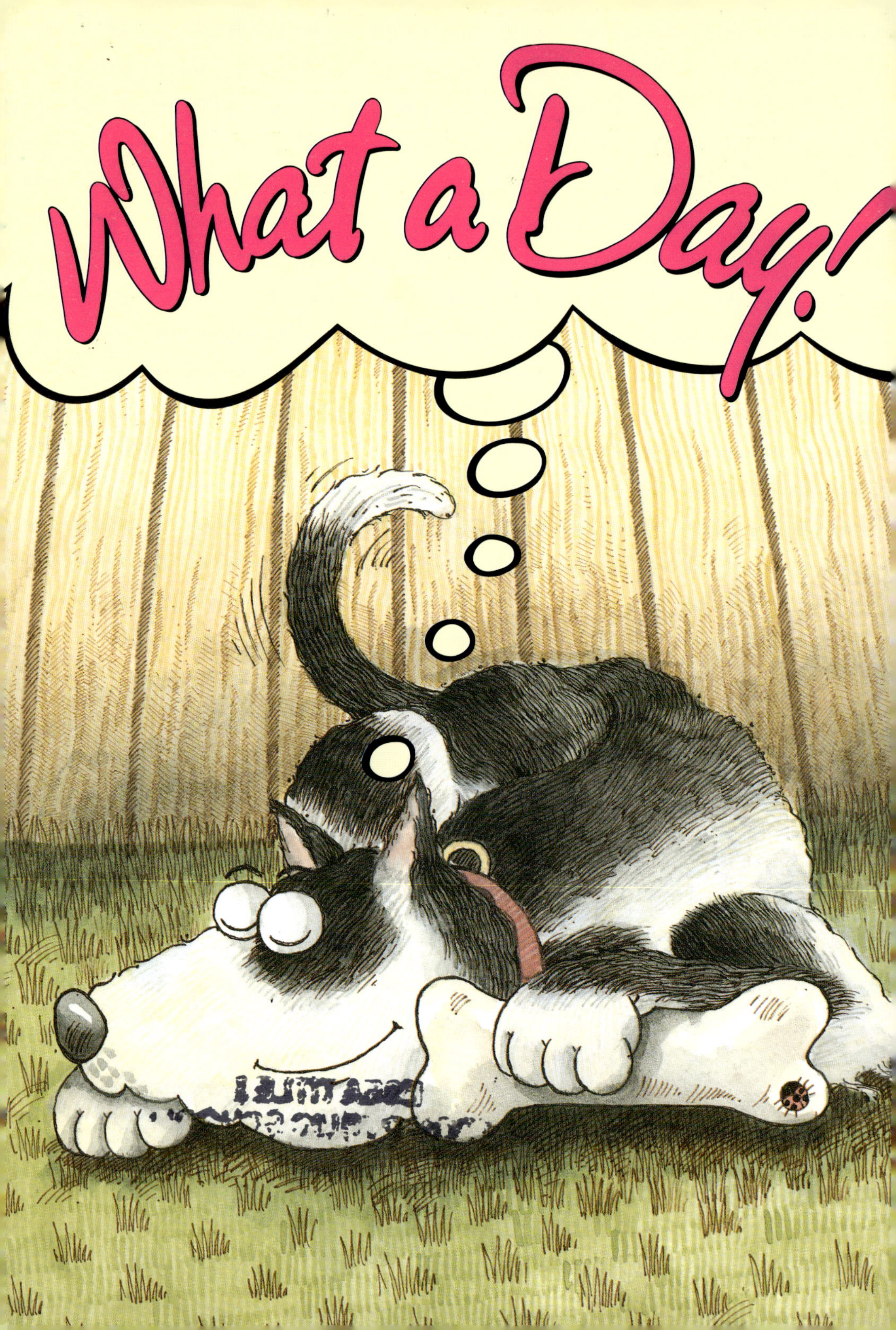
What a Day!